THE HALLOWEEN JOKES GAME BOOK FOR KIDS

INTERACTIVE EDITION

Copyright 2020 by Hayden Fox - All rights reserved.

This document is geared towards providing exact and reliable information in regards to the topic and issue covered. The publication is sold with the idea that the publisher is not required to render an accounting, officially permitted, or otherwise, qualified services. If advice is necessary, legal or professional, a practiced individual in the profession should be ordered.

- From a Declaration of Principles which was accepted and approved equally by a Committee of the American Bar Association and a Committee of Publishers and Associations.

In no way is it legal to reproduce, duplicate, or transmit any part of this document by either electronic means or in printed format. Recording of this publication is strictly prohibited and any storage of this document is not allowed unless with written permission from the publisher. All rights reserved.

The information provided herein is stated to be truthful and consistent, in that any liability, in terms of inattention or otherwise, by any usage or abuse of any policies, processes, or directions contained within is the solitary and utter responsibility of the recipient reader. Under no circumstances will any legal responsibility or blame be held against the publisher for any reparation, damages, or monetary loss due to the information herein, either directly or indirectly.

Respective authors and companies own all copyrights not held by the publisher.

The information herein is offered for informational purposes solely and is universal as so. The presentation of the information is without a contract or any type of guarantee assurance.

The trademarks that are used are without any consent, and the publication of the trademark is without permission or backing by the trademark owner. All trademarks and brands within this book are for clarifying purposes only and are owned by the owners themselves, not affiliated with this document.

How To Play

Step 1

SPLIT INTO TWO TEAMS WHETHER THAT BE BOYS VS GIRLS, KIDS VS PARENTS, OR ANY MIX OF YOUR CHOICE. IF POSSIBLE, ALSO ASSIGN ONE PERSON AS A REFEREE. YOU CAN ALSO DO 1 VS 1!

Step 2

DECIDE WHO GETS TO GO FIRST. WHICH TEAM CAN DO THE MOST PUSHUPS? WHICH TEAM CAN GUESS THE NUMBER BETWEEN 1 AND 10 FROM SOMEONE NOT PLAYING THE GAME? OR JUST A GOOD OLD FASHIONED ROCK PAPER SCISSORS?

Step 3

THE STARTING TEAM HAS TO TELL A JOKE FROM THE BOOK. YOU CAN SAY THE JOKE HOWEVER YOU LIKE AND ANIMATE IT TOO WITH FUNNY FACES, GESTURES, OR WHATEVER ELSE.

Step 4

IF EVERYONE ON THE OPPOSING TEAM LAUGHS, THE OTHER TEAM GETS A POINT! SET A LIMIT FOR HOW MANY POINTS IT TAKES TO WIN AND THE FIRST TEAM TO REACH THE LIMIT, WINS!

WHY DID THE ZOMBIE GO NUTS?

Because he lost his mind!

WHY DID THE ZOMBIE COMEDIAN GET BOOED OFF STAGE?

Because all his jokes were rotten!

WHY DIDN'T THE ZOMBIE GET THE ROLE IN THE MOVIE?

The director wanted someone more lively!

WHY DID THE ZOMBIE JOIN THE ARMY?

He heard they gave out arms!

WHAT DID THE ZOMBIE SAY AFTER EATING THE COMEDIAN?

This tastes funny!

WHAT KIND OF VEHICLES DO MUMMIES DRIVE?

Monster trucks!

WHAT CANDY DO GHOULS HATE THE MOST?
Life Savers

WHAT'S A BABY ZOMBIE'S FAVORITE TOY?
A deady bear

WHERE DO BABY ZOMBIES GO DURING THE DAY?

Dayscare centres

WHO DID THE ZOMBIE TAKE WITH HIM TO THE PROM?

His ghoul friend

WHO WON THE SKELETON BEAUTY CONTEST?

Nobody

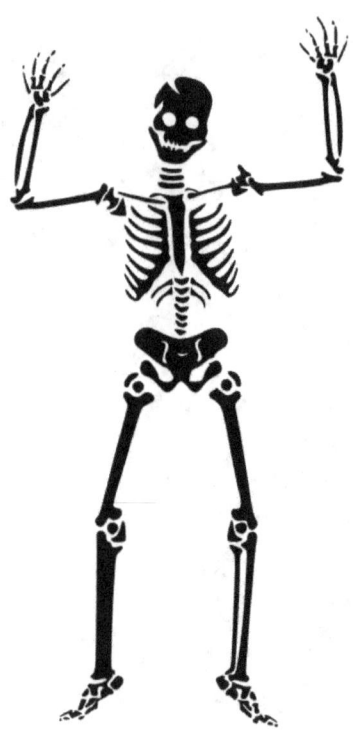

WHAT DO SKELETONS SAY BEFORE EATING?

Bone appetit!

WHAT DO GHOSTS LIKE WITH THEIR COFFEE?

Scream and sugar

WHAT IS A MONSTER'S FAVORITE DESSERT?

I scream

WHAT IS A SCARECROW'S FAVORITE FRUIT?
Straw-berries

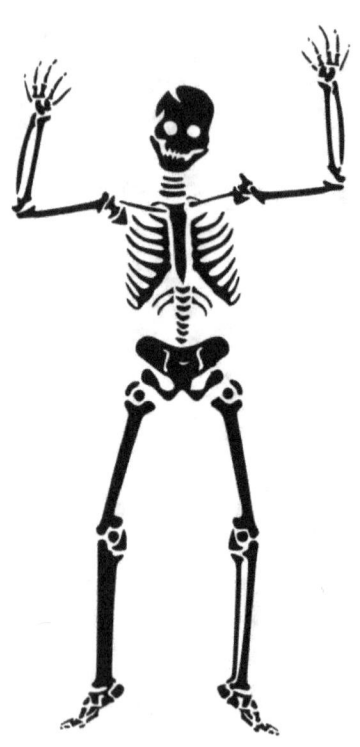

WHAT HAPPENS WHEN A VAMPIRE GETS LOST IN THE FOG?
He is mist.

WHAT ROOM IN THE HOUSE DOES A ZOMBIE NOT NEED?

The living room

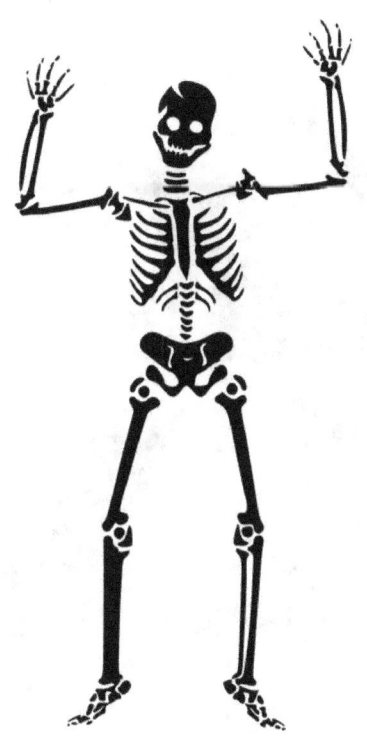

WHEN IS IT BAD LUCK TO BE FOLLOWED BY A BLACK CAT?

When you're a mouse!

WHAT HAPPENS IF A VAMPIRE STAYS IN THE SNOW TOO LONG?

Frostbite

WHAT'S BIG AND SCARY AND HAS 3 WHEELS?

A monster riding a tricycle!

WHAT POSITION DO ZOMBIES PLAY IN HOCKEY?

Ghoulie

WHAT DO YOU CALL A WITCH THAT GOES TO THE BEACH?

A sandwitch

WHAT DO GHOSTS LIKE TO PUT IN THEIR PANCAKES?

Boonanas and Booberries

WHAT ROADS DO GHOSTS LIKE TO HAUNT?

Dead ends

WHAT KIND OF COOKIES DO MONSTERS PREFER?

Ghoul scout cookies

WHAT KIND OF CANDY DO VAMPIRES ENJOY THE MOST?

Suckers

WHAT DO GHOSTS LIKE TO EAT FOR DINNER?

Spookghetti

WHAT DO MONSTERS LIKE ON THEIR SUNDAES?

Whipped scream

WHAT SONG DOES DRACULA HATE THE MOST?

You Are My Sunshine

WHAT MONSTER LOVES DANCE MUSIC?

The Boogieman

WHY DO GHOSTS LIKE GOING OUT SO MUCH?

Because they love to boo-gie!

WHERE DO MOST OF THE WEREWOLVES LIVE?

Howllywood, California

WHAT KIND OF MAKEUP DO GHOSTS WEAR?

Mas-scare-a

WHO IS THE MOST FAMOUS GHOST DETECTIVE TO EVER LIVE?

Sherlock Moans

WHY DID THE VAMPIRE NEED COLD MEDICINE?

In order to stop coffin!

WHY DOESN'T ANYONE LIKE DRACULA?

Because he has a bat temper!

WHO DOES DRACULA GET LETTERS FROM?
From his fang club

WHAT CAN'T YOU GIVE THE HEADLESS HORSEMAN?
A headache

WHAT DO YOU CALL A LITTLE MONSTER'S PARENTS?

Mummy and Deady

WHAT HAPPENED WHEN TWO VAMPIRES WENT OUT ON A BLIND DATE?

It was love at first bite!

WHERE DO GHOSTS LIKE TO GO ON VACATION?
Mali-boo

WHERE DO WEREWOLVES STORE THEIR BELONGINGS?
In a were-house

WHAT KIND OF TREAT IS NEVER ON TIME?
ChocoLATE

WHAT DO THE MONSTERS USE TO CLEAN THE ICE AFTER HOCKEY GAMES?
A Zombieoni

WHAT KIND OF MISTAKES DO GHOSTS MAKE?

Boo boos

WHAT AMUSEMENT PARK RIDE DO GHOSTS LIKE THE MOST?

Roller ghosters

HOW CAN MONSTERS TELL THEIR FUTURES?

By reading their horrorscopes!

WHY CAN'T YOU SEE A GHOST'S MOTHER AND FATHER?

Because they're transparents!

WHAT KIND OF MUSIC DO GHOSTS LISTEN TO?

Spiritual music

WHY DIDN'T THE SKELETON CROSS THE ROAD?

He didn't have the guts

WHAT DO MONKEY GHOSTS LIKE TO EAT?

Boonanas

WHAT DOES IT TAKE TO BECOME A VAMPIRE?

Deadication

WHAT SPORT DO VAMPIRES LIKE THE MOST?

Batminton

WHY DID THE ZOMBIE QUIT HIS TEACHING JOB?

Because he only had 1 pupil left!

HOW ARE ZOMBIES LIKE COMPUTERS?
They both have megabites!

WHERE DO ZOMBIES GO ON VACATION?
To the Deaditerranean

WHO WON THE ZOMBIE RACE?
Nobody. It was DEAD even!

WHAT DOES A ZOMBIE GET WHEN HE'S LATE FOR A DATE?
The cold shoulder

WHAT IS A MUMMY'S FAVORITE SHAKESPEARE PLAY?

Romeo and Ghouliette

WHAT'S DRACULA'S FAVORITE PET?

His bloodhound

WHAT DO YOU GET FROM CROSSING BAMBI AND A GHOST?

Bamboo

WHICH ONE OF COUNT DRACULA'S RELATIVES HAS A BILL AND WEBBED FEET?

Count Duckula

WHAT DOES TWEETY SAY WHEN TRICK OR TREATING?

Twick or tweet

WHAT DO WITCHES USE TO KEEP THEIR HAIR IN PLACE?

Scare spray

WHAT MEDICINE DO YOU GIVE TO A VAMPIRE WITH A COLD?

Coffin Drops

HOW DO YOU FIX A BROKEN JACK-O-LANTERN?

By using a pumpkin patch.

WHEN DOES A SKELETON LAUGH?

When someone tickles its funny bone.

WHERE DO GHOSTS MAIL THEIR LETTERS?

At the ghost office.!

WHERE DO GHOSTS GO SHOPPING FOR FOOD?

At the ghost-ery store!

WHAT HAPPENED TO THE GUY THAT DIDN'T PAY HIS EXORCIST?

He got repossessed!

WHAT DO GHOSTS EAT FOR LUNCH?
Boo-logna sandwiches

WHAT IS A WITCH'S FAVORITE SUBJECT IN SCHOOL?
Spell-ing

WHAT DO SKELETONS ORDER AT RESTAURANTS?

Spare ribs

WHERE DID THE GOBLIN THROW THE FOOTBALL?

Over the ghoul line.

WHY WAS THE MUMMY SO TENSE?
Because he was all wound up!

WHY DO WITCHES WEAR NAME TAGS?
So they know which witch is which.

WHAT DO GHOSTS MAIL HOME WHEN ON VACATION?

Ghostcards

WHY DID THE WITCH STOP TELLING FORTUNES?

Because there was no future in it!

WHAT DO YOU CALL TWO WITCHES SHARING THE SAME ROOM?

Broom mates

WHAT DO VAMPIRES FEAR THE MOST?

Tooth decay

WHY ARE GHOSTS SUCH TERRIBLE LIARS?

Because you can see right through them!

WHAT IS DRACULA'S FAVORITE BUILDING IN NEW YORK CITY?

The Vampire State Building

WHAT DID THE BAT SAY TO HIS GIRLFRIEND?

I like to hang out with you!

WHAT'S A VAMPIRE'S LEAST FAVORITE FOOD?

Stake

WHAT GENRE OF MUSIC DO MUMMIES LIKE?

Wrap music

HOW DO GHOSTS WASH THEIR HAIR?

With shamboo

WHICH MONSTER LIKES TO PLAY TRICKS ON HALLOWEEN?

Prankenstein

WHY COULDN'T THE SKELETON SCORE ANY GOALS?

Because he had no heart.

WHY DID THE ZOMBIE SKIP SCHOOL?
Because he felt rotten inside!.

WHAT DID THE CAT SAY TO HER BOYFRIEND ON HALLOWEEN?
You're purr-fect for me.

WHAT IS A GHOST'S NOSE FULL OF?
Boooogers

WHAT DO BIRDS LIKE TO SAY ON HALLOWEEN?
Trick or tweet

WHAT CANDY DO YOU EAT ON THE PLAYGROUND?

Recess pieces

WHAT INSTRUMENT DOES A SKELETON PLAY?

The trombone

WHEN DO GHOULS LIKE TO COOK THEIR VICTIMS?

On Fry Day

WHEN DOES A GHOST HAVE BREAKFAST?

In the moaning

WHERE DO VAMPIRES USUALLY EAT LUNCH?

At the casketeria.

WHAT DO ZOMBIES LIKE TO DRINK ON A HOT SUMMER DAY?

Ghoul-aid

WHERE DO MOST GOBLINS LIVE?
North and South Scarolina

WHERE CAN YOU FIND A WITCH'S GARAGE?
In the broom closet!

WHAT DO OWLS SAY WHEN THEY GO TRICK OR TREATING?

Happy Owl-ween!

WHY DID THE GHOST GO INTO THE BAR?

To get some boos!

WHO ARE A WEREWOLF'S COUSINS?

What-wolf, who-wolf, when-wolf and how-wolf!

WHAT GROWS IN THE GARDENS ON HALLOWEEN?

Zombeets

WHY CAN'T SKELETON MUSICIANS PERFORM AT CHURCH?

Because they have no organs!

WHO DO COWBOY ZOMBIES FIGHT?

The Deadskins

WHY DON'T PEOPLE LIKE VAMPIRES?
They have bat tempers!

WHAT WAS THE MUMMY MUSICIAN'S FAVORITE NOTE?
The dead sea

WHAT DO WEREWOLVES READ TO THEIR CHILDREN BEFORE SLEEPING?

Hairy tails

WHY DO WITCHES RIDE BROOMS?

Because the vacuum cleaner's power chord is too short!

HOW DO VAMPIRES FLIRT?
They bat their eyes!

WHERE DID THE ZOMBIE THROW THE FOOTBALL?
Over the ghoul line!

WHY WAS THE GHOST ARRESTED FOR SCARING YOUNGSTERS?

Because he didn't have a haunting license!

WHAT DO YOU CALL A GHOST WHO GETS TOO CLOSE TO THE FIRE?

A toasty ghosty

WHY WAS THE GHOUL SUCH A MESSY EATER?

Because he was always goblin!

WHAT DO YOU CALL A MONSTER WITH A BROKEN LEG?

Hoblin Goblin

WHAT DID THE SKELETON SAY WHEN HE WAS RIDING HIS HARLEY?

I'm bone to be wild!

WHY DO VAMPIRES THINK THEY ARE GOOD ARTISTS?

Because they like to draw blood!

WHO DID THE GHOUL INVITE TO HIS BIRTHDAY PARTY?

Anyone he could dig up!

WHAT IS A VAMPIRE'S FAVORITE FOOD?

Blood orange

WHAT IS A PIRATE ALWAYS LOOKING FOR EVEN THOUGH IT'S RIGHT BEHIND HIM?

Booty

HOW COME THE PIRATE BOUGHT HIS EARRING AT THE DOLLAR STORE?

Because it was a buck-an-ear!

WHAT'S A VAMPIRE'S FAVORITE FRUIT?
Nectarine

WHAT'S A VAMPIRE'S FAVORITE ANIMAL?
A giraffe

WHY DIDN'T ANYONE WANT TO LOOK AFTER THE BABY VAMPIRE?

Because he was a pain in the neck!

WHY DO VAMPIRES NEED MOUTHWASH?

Because they have bat breath!

HOW DO YOU JOIN A VAMPIRE FAN CLUB?

By submitting your name, address, phone number and blood type!

IF TWO WITCHES WOULD WATCH TWO WATCHES, WHICH WITCH WOULD WATCH WHICH WATCH?

HOW IS A WITCH'S FACE LIKE A MILLION DOLLARS?

Both are green and wrinkly.

CREEPY CRAWLING CRITTERS CRAWL CARELESSLY THROUGH CRAZY CREEPY CORRIDORS.

WHAT IS THE RATIO OF A PUMPKIN'S CIRCUMFERENCE TO ITS DIAMETER?

Pumpkin pi

HOW CAN YOU TELL A VAMPIRE HAS BEEN IN A BAKERY?

All the jelly has been sucked out of the jelly doughnuts!

WHY DID THE HEADLESS HORSEMAN START A BUSINESS?

He wanted to get a-head in life!

WHY DON'T ANGRY WITCHES RIDE THEIR BROOMS?

They're afraid of flying off the handle!

WHAT PANTS DO GHOSTS WEAR?
Boojeans

WHAT IS A GHOST'S FAVORITE GAME?
Hide-and-ghost-seek

WHAT IS A GHOST'S FAVORITE CANDY?

Booble gum.

WHY ARE VAMPIRES EASY TO FOOL?

Because they are suckers!

SEVEN SPINDLY SPIDERS SPIN SPOOKY SILK SPEEDILY

HORRIBLY HOARSE HOOT OWLS HOOT HOWLS OF HORROR IN HALLOWEEN HAUNTED HOUSES

PROFESSIONAL PUMPKIN PICKERS ARE PRONE TO PICK THE PLUMPEST PUMPKINS

CREEPY CRAWLER CRITTERS CRAWL THROUGH CREEPY CRAWLY CRATERS

IF BIG BLACK BATS COULD BLOW BUBBLES, HOW BIG OF BUBBLES WOULD BIG BLACK BATS BLOW?

TRANSYLVANIAN TREE TRIMMERS ARE TRAINED TO TRIM THE TALLEST TRANSYLVANIAN TREES.

Knock Knock!

Who's there?

Ice Cream.

Ice cream who?

Ice cream every time I see a ghost!

Knock Knock!!

Who's there?

Boo.

Boo Who?

Ah, don't cry, Halloween is just around the corner!

Knock, Knock!!

Who's there?

Ivan.

Ivan who?

Ivan to suck your blood!!

Knock, Knock!!

Who's there?

Frank.

Frank who?

Frankenstein!

Knock, Knock!!

Who's there?

Howl!

Howl who?

Howl you be dressing up this Halloween?

Knock, Knock!!

Who's there?

Phillip.

Phillip who?

Phillip my bag with Halloween candy!

Knock, Knock!!

Who's there?

Olive.

Olive who?

Olive Halloween!

Knock, Knock!!

Who's there?

Voodoo!

Voodoo who?

Voodoo you think you are!

Knock, Knock!!

Who's there?

Jacklyn.

Jacklyn who?

Jacklyn Hyde!

Knock, Knock!!

Who's there?

Iran!

Iran who?

Iran over here to get some candy!

HAPPY HALLOWEEN!

Thank you for reading! We hope everyone enjoyed the book and had lots of laughs.

As a special bonus, enjoy this exclusive preview of one our other popular titles!

Would You Rather Book for Kids

A Hilariously Fun Activity Book for the Entire Family

How to Play

Step 1

Split into two teams whether that be boys vs girls, kids vs parents, or any mix of your choice. If possible, also assign one person as a referee.

Step 2

Decide who gets to go first. Which team can do the most pushups? Which team can guess the number between 1 and 10 from someone not playing the game? Or just some good old fashioned rock paper scissors?

Step 3

The starting team has to ask a question from the book and the opposing team has 10 seconds to not only choose an option but to also give a meaningful reason as to why they chose what they did. The referee decides whether the answer is acceptable.

Step 4

The team can discuss their answer together but only one player can give the answer. The person answering has to alternate every turn.

Step 5

If the player who is answering can't choose or give a good reason then that player is out for the game and can't answer anymore or be involved in the team discussion.

Step 6

Repeat until all players are eliminated.

Step 7 (optional)

Decide whether it will be a single game or best of 3, 5 or 7.

Let's begin!

WOULD YOU RATHER...

> Be a superhero
>
> -OR-
>
> a wizard?

> Have the ability to fly
>
> -OR-
>
> read minds?

WOULD YOU RATHER...

Lick the floor

-OR-

lick someone's armpit?

Be a cat

-OR-

a dog?

WOULD YOU RATHER...

Fall into a puddle of mud

-OR-

a pile of yellow snow?

Do 100 pushups

-OR-

100 situps?

WOULD YOU RATHER...

Get yelled at by Mom

-OR-

by Dad?

Run 10 miles

-OR-

bike 50 miles?

A Message From the Publisher

Hello! My name is Hayden and I am the owner of Hayden Fox Publishing, the publishing house that brought you this title.

My hope is that you enjoyed this book and had some fun and laughs on every page. If you did, please think about leaving a review for us on Amazon or wherever you purchased this book. It may only take a moment, but it really does mean the world for small businesses like mine.

Our mission is to create premium content for children that will help them build confidence, grow their imaginations, get away from screens, spend more quality time with family, and have lots of fun and laughs doing it. Without you, however, this would not be possible, so we sincerely thank you for your purchase and for supporting our company mission.

~ Hayden

Check out our other books!

For more, visit our Amazon store at:
amazon.com/author/haydenfox

www.ingramcontent.com/pod-product-compliance
Lightning Source LLC
Chambersburg PA
CBHW071252070526
44583CB00017B/2432